POLITICAL
LONDON

POLITICAL LONDON

A Guide to the Capital's
Political Sights

J B Seatrobe

First published in Great Britain 2000
Published by Politico's Publishing
8 Artillery Row
Westminster
London
SW1P 1RZ
Tel 020 7931 0090
Fax 020 7828 8111
Email publishing@politicos.co.uk
Website http://www.politicos.co.uk/publishing

A catalogue record of this book is available from the British Library.
ISBN 1 902301 52 8

Printed and bound in Great Britain by St. Edmundsbury Press.
Cover Design by Advantage

Contents

Preface

This book is dedicated to the political sights and sites of London. There seem to be books about all imaginable aspects of London, but not one devoted solely to the metropolis as a capital city, seat of government, home of parliaments, refuge for political exiles from all over the world, and stage for some of the greatest political dramas in history.

Whether you are a tourist, interested in the rich political life and history of this great city, or a true political anorak eager to stand on the site of great events or outside the places where the famous have lived and worked, *Political London* is the book for you.

Political London isn't an A–Z listing of places and streets. It's a guide presented in various ways and themes to provide you with a genuine feel of the political life and history of London.

Deep gratitude is owed to Shona and Keith Skakle, without whose valuable research assistance and advice this book would have been much the poorer. Grateful thanks also go to Geoff Lindsey for his input. The enthusiasm and guidance of the staff at Politico's more than made up for their tight publishing deadlines! John Simmons provided the 'Political eating, drinking and shopping' section and compiled the index.

Responsibility for any errors rests as always with the author, who welcomes any suggestions and additions for future editions of *Political London*.

JBS

March 2000

POLITICAL HOT SPOTS

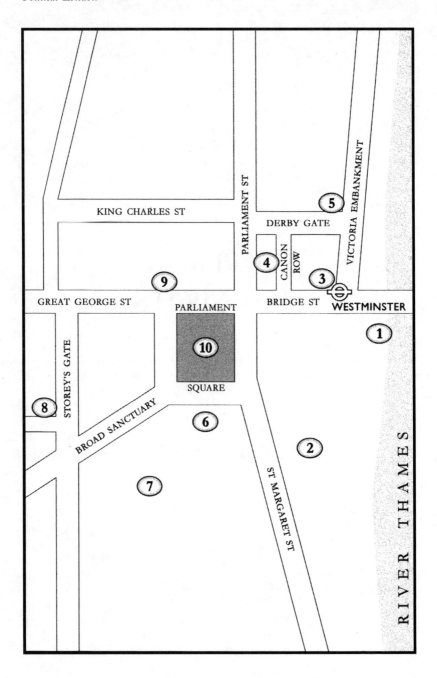

KING CHARLES ST

PARLIAMENT ST

DERBY GATE

VICTORIA EMBANKMENT

⑤

④ CANON ROW

③

⑨

GREAT GEORGE ST

BRIDGE ST

WESTMINSTER

①

PARLIAMENT

⑩

STOREY'S GATE

SQUARE

⑧

BROAD SANCTUARY

⑥

⑦

②

ST MARGARET ST

RIVER THAMES

Parliament Square

The area around Parliament Square brings together much of Britain's political and parliamentary history. The government buildings in Whitehall are to the north, the Houses of Parliament to the east and Westminster Abbey immediately to the south.

1. PALACE OF WESTMINSTER

A Gothic building facing the river, home to the two Houses of Parliament, the Commons to the north and the Lords to the south. If Parliament is sitting, there will be a 'Union Jack' flying over the Victoria Tower and, after dark, a light will be on at the top of the Clock Tower ('Big Ben'). Although access to the Palace is now generally strictly controlled, people can queue outside the St Stephen's entrance to listen to debates, and there are also guided tours by arrangement. Write to your MP at the House of Commons, London SW1A 0AA, or foreign visitors can apply to the Parliamentary Education Unit, Norman Shaw Building North, London SW1A 2TT (020 7219 4272).

Westminster Bridge or the riverbank opposite are the best places to see the front of

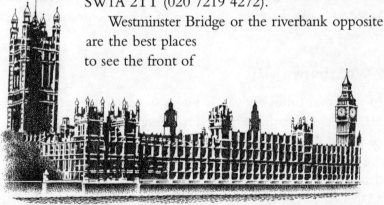

the Palace in all its glory, especially the riverfront terrace where MPs, peers and their guests congregate when the weather permits.

Parliamentarians can be seen coming and going through the large Carriage Gates into New Palace Yard, especially around 7pm and 10pm when there are likely to be votes. On Wednesday afternoons the Prime Minister is driven in on the way to the weekly half-hour of PM's Question Time. Most spectacular of all is the State Opening of Parliament, usually in November each year.

The House of Lords Record Office lives in the Victoria Tower, at the southern end of the Palace. This repository of the parliamentary archives includes original Acts of Parliament. The Office is open to the public, who can examine documents in the Search Room.

The Houses of Parliament have not been free of political violence. Apart from the 1605 Gunpowder Plot, the Prime Minister, Spencer Perceval, was shot dead in the lobby of the House of Commons on 11 May 1812. There was a bomb attack on Westminster Hall by Fenians in 1885 which caused a large hole in the floor, and the Conservative MP, Airey Neave, was killed by a car bomb on the ramp of the underground car park in New Palace Yard on 30 March 1979.

2. WESTMINSTER HALL

In medieval times, Royal or Great Councils were held in the Hall, although Parliament itself has never met there, as such. For centuries Westminster Hall was the seat of English justice with the law courts sited there. Other notable political or state occasions in the Hall include the trials of Sir Thomas More in 1535, Guy Fawkes in 1606, Thomas Wentworth, Earl of

Strafford, Charles I's Minister, in 1641, Charles I himself in January 1649, and Warren Hastings from 1788 to 1795. The last impeachment there was that of Viscount Melville in 1806, who was acquitted.

Westminster Hall has seen the lying in state of major figures, such as Gladstone in June 1898 and Churchill in January 1965. It was the scene of addresses to both Houses by heads of state – Presidents Lebrun and De Gaulle of France in 1939 and 1960 respectively, and by President Mandela of South Africa in July 1996.

The Hall is still used for important public events, such as the celebration of Winston Churchill's 80th birthday (including presentation of the notorious Sutherland portrait) on 30 November 1954; the 700th anniversary of Simon de Montfort's Parliament in 1965; the tercentenary of the Glorious Revolution in 1988, and the 50th anniversary of the United Nations in 1995.

3. PORTCULLIS HOUSE

The newest of the parliamentary buildings, constructed above the rebuilt Westminster tube station, it provides office space for over 200 MPs and their staff on seven floors, with committee rooms and other common facilities.

4. PARLIAMENT STREET BLOCK

A series of buildings which were incorporated as parliamentary accommodation in 1991. At the Bridge Street corner is the Parliamentary Bookshop. Between it and Canon Row was St Stephen's Tavern, a popular watering hole for politicians. The corner site had occupants from the National Labour Committee to the Department of Transport. Looking north up Parliament Street is the main parliamentary entrance, 1 Parliament Street, in what was formerly nos. 34-42. No. 38 was occupied by the notorious Maundy Gregory (see *Scandals*). Nos 2 and 3, formerly 43-44, were the residences for parliamentarians, offices for parliamentary clerks, and for several government bodies. No. 43 was for a time a Liberal Party office, and no. 44 was well-known as a post office for parliamentarians and tourists alike. At the north end of the block is 1 Derby Gate, formerly nos. 45-47 Parliament Street, now housing much of the House of Commons Library. No. 47 was for forty years the Whitehall Club, and from 1966 to 1972, the Welsh Office.

5. NORMAN SHAW BUILDINGS

These much-filmed buildings, designed by Richard Norman Shaw (1890) formerly housed the HQ of the Metropolitan Police, 'New Scotland Yard', after their move from the original Scotland Yard, further up Whitehall. Nowadays, as Norman Shaw North and Norman Shaw South, they are used as MPs' offices.

6. ST MARGARET'S CHURCH

This church is commonly known as the Parish Church of the House of Commons. Its parliamentary connection probably began with a Palm Sunday service for the whole House in 1614, a practice which lasted half a century. The Church is often used for major national occasions, such as services of thanksgiving after the two world wars in the twentieth century. A service is held at the beginning of each new parliament, and the church hosts numerous religious services for Members and their families, from weddings to memorial services.

7. WESTMINSTER ABBEY

In the Abbey are buried some of Britain's most illustrious political figures, including no less than eight Prime Ministers. Others include Wilberforce, Fox, Ernest Bevin and Beatrice and Sidney Webb. There are many statues and memorials to other political notables, including Asquith, Peel and Disraeli.

8. CENTRAL HALL, WESTMINSTER

Built early last century as the Methodist Church's HQ, it became a convenient location for public events and political meetings. Many famous political figures have spoken here, including Lloyd George (attempting one of his comebacks in 1935) and foreign leaders such as de Gaulle, Gandhi and Gorbachev. Labour and Conservative party conferences were held here during both world wars. It was also the venue for a special Labour conference on Common Market entry in July 1971.

Perhaps Central Hall's finest hour was in early 1946 with the inaugural meeting of the General Assembly of the United Nations. Ernest Bevin, the Foreign Secretary, had to persuade the Hall's trustees that the UN meeting should be held there. Even so, the availability of a bar for the delegates upset the Methodist Church. The General Assembly first met on 10 January 1946. The Labour Prime Minister, Clement Attlee, unveiled a commemorative plaque on 28 May 1946.

9. GREAT GEORGE STREET

Its close proximity to Parliament made this a popular residential street for MPs and peers. George Grenville lived there; John Wilkes lived at no. 13 between 1757 and 1763, and Sir Robert Peel at no. 36 in 1813. The architect of the new Houses of Parliament, Sir Charles Barry, lived at no. 32 between 1859 and 1870. The north side of the street disappeared in 1910 when what is now the vast Treasury building was constructed.

10. PARLIAMENT SQUARE

The Square is filled with political statues, from that of Churchill (unveiled by Lady Spencer Churchill, 1973) to those of the Victorian premiers Peel (1850), Derby (1874), Palmerston (1876) and Disraeli (1883). Next to the Lincoln statue is Canning Green, named after the Tory PM, George Canning. Canning's statue (erected in 1832, at a cost of £7,000) originally stood nearer Westminster Hall, but was moved in 1867 when alterations were made to the layout of the area. Although there are strict laws about assemblies close to Parliament, the Square often hosts protest demonstrations by those keen to publicise their case with parliamentarians.

Whitehall

Whitehall is known as the centre of British government, even though many government offices have been dispersed. It's not just Downing Street, the Cenotaph, the state occasions and the massive piles housing the Ministry of Defence, the Treasury and the Foreign Office. It's also its long history,

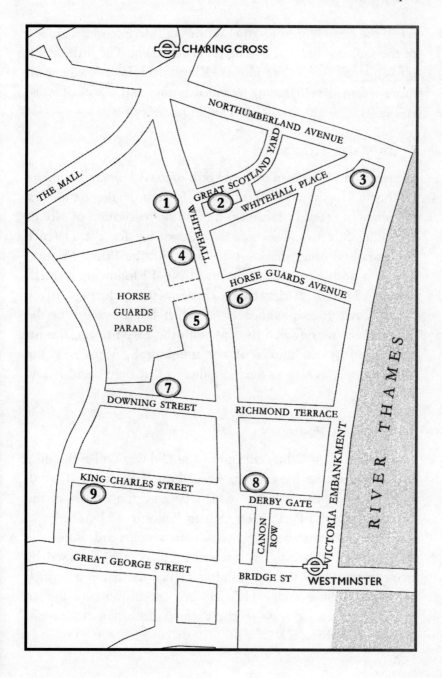

when the sprawling, long-gone Whitehall Palace (covering much of the site) was the seat of English government. The little streets off Whitehall (some, like historic King Street, now lost beneath more recent development) provided homes and places of work and entertainment for all involved in matters of state.

1. ADMIRALTY HOUSE

Its apartments were used by First Lords of the Admiralty (including Balfour and Churchill) until 1960. It became the temporary residence of Harold Macmillan during the renovation of No. 10 Downing Street, and is used as a residence for the Defence Secretary and other ministers. In the 1990s the Prime Minister operated from here during repairs at No 10 following terrorist attacks. This had disastrous consequences during 'Black Wednesday', 16 September 1992, when key members of the government were forced to cope with the ERM financial crisis with virtually no means of communication. Apparently the Chief Whip was sent to fetch a radio, so that they could follow events!

2. WHITEHALL PLACE

It is flanked at the Whitehall end by the Old War Office Building and offices of the Ministry of Agriculture, Fisheries and Food. No. 4 was a private house, which became the offices of the commissioners of Peel's Metropolitan Police in 1829. The back, used as a police station, opened on to a courtyard, known as 'Scotland Yard', because it was on a site of a house used by Scottish monarchs visiting London. Hence the name by which the Metropolitan Police HQ has become immortalised, even when it moved in 1890 to the Victoria Embankment, and in 1967 to Broadway, SW1.

3. NATIONAL LIBERAL CLUB

No. 1 Whitehall Place is better known as the National Liberal Club, formed in 1882 with Gladstone as its first President. In 1916 the Club was pressed into war duties. The Liberal Party and the European Movement have had their headquarters on the premises.

4. 36 WHITEHALL

This modest building is a good example of the political history of Whitehall. In the 17th century the Office of the Paymaster of the Forces was on the site. The present building was constructed in the 1730s, with additions in 1806. Following restoration (after wartime bomb damage) involving new internal offices within the retained facades, the building was occupied by the Parliamentary Counsel Office. There is a reconstruction of the historic Paymaster General's room on the ground floor.

5. DOVER HOUSE

Built in the 1750s, it became the French Ambassador's home, and later York House (1788-92 when the Duke of York lived there). When the Duke exchanged it for Lord Melbourne's Piccadilly house, it was renamed Melbourne House between 1793-1830, and then became Dover House. It was offered to Gladstone, when PM, as an alternative to Downing Street, but he refused because he feared that its grandeur compared to No. 10 would require him to hold more social events, destroying his privacy. It was occupied by the Scottish Office in 1885, remaining in Scottish hands thereafter, even after devolution. Across Whitehall is Gwydyr House, the Welsh Office.

6. BANQUETING HOUSE

The last surviving remnant of Whitehall Palace, it dates from the early 1620s. As the plaque on a bust of Charles I above the entrance notes, it was here that the unfortunate monarch was beheaded on 30 January 1649. It is used for major occasions, such as the lunch on 20 November 1997, where the Prime Minister, Tony Blair, made a speech celebrating the golden wedding anniversary of the Queen and the Duke of Edinburgh. It is the only major building in Whitehall open to the public, and there is a fascinating picture in the entrance showing a proposed seating plan, dated 7 November 1936, for the possible wedding and coronation of Edward VIII.

7. DOWNING STREET

A short, narrow street, it is probably the best-known road in Britain, with No. 10, No. 11 (the official residence of the Chancellor of the Exchequer) and No. 12 (the office of the Government Chief Whip). No. 10, with one of the world's most recognisable front doors (actually there are two, to allow for repairs and renovation), is the Prime Minister's official residence, by virtue of being First Lord of the Treasury. The brass plaque on the door proclaims 'First

Lord of the Treasury', and when various PMs, such as Churchill, asked that the plaque be removed, they were told that they would have to pay rent for living there as Prime Minister.

Robert Walpole, Britain's first Prime Minister, was offered No. 10 by George II in 1732, and moved in three years later. Since then, most premiers have lived there when in office. No. 10 is not as small as it may appear from its Downing Street frontage. It has over 160 rooms, and it is actually two linked houses, one (Albemarle House, later Bothmar House) being a large three-storey property facing Horse Guards Parade.

The street was so named by George Downing, who had a varied career, from public official to MP during the 17th century. He acquired property west of Whitehall, which he demolished and built the houses in the street. Of the original development, only Nos. 10 and 11 remain; No. 12 was totally remodelled in the 1960s. The street used to be accessible to the public, and was regularly filled with tourists, some perhaps emulating the eight-year-old Harold Wilson, who, in 1924, had his photo taken outside No. 10. Because of the terrorist threat, the street was closed to the public in the 1980s, a security barrier was put up in 1981, and a set of gates were erected in 1989-90, which remain to this day.

8. THE RED LION PUBLIC HOUSE

This is one of the surviving reminders of the dozens of drinking places which were dotted around Whitehall. It is on the site of a medieval tavern. The present pub was rebuilt in 1900, and is a regular haunt of parliamentarians.

9. CABINET WAR ROOMS

The fortified shelter for Winston Churchill, his Cabinet and senior military and intelligence advisers during World War II. The various rooms where they lived and worked have been open to the public for a number of years.

Smith Square

The area around Smith Square is full of political interest, and, in conjunction with Parliament itself, helps make 'Westminster' the generic name for parliamentary and party political activity. Conservative Central Office has been in the Square since 1958; Labour's HQ was Transport House, 1928-1980, and the Liberals' HQ was in the Square for a time in the 1960s.

1. SMITH SQUARE

It's not just Transport House and Conservative Central Office (at no. 32) which make Smith Square 'political'. The leading Conservative, Rab Butler lived for a time at no. 3, west of Lord North Street, until it was bombed in 1940, and the fascist leader, Sir Oswald Mosley lived at nos. 8-9, to the east of the street. Many connected with local political life dine in the Footstool restaurant in St John's Church in the centre of the Square.

2. TRANSPORT HOUSE

Designed as the HQ of the newly formed Transport and General Workers Union, it was intentionally located near Parliament and Government. In 1925, it was agreed that the TUC and the

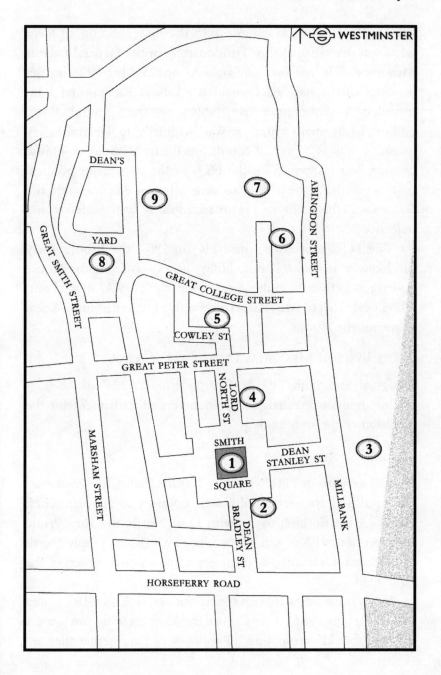

Labour Party would also move into the new building, to form what was described as the "Headquarters of the General Labour Movement". It was formally opened on 15 May 1928, in the presence of Ramsay MacDonald, the Labour Party leader, who unveiled a commemorative tablet on the ground floor. Although the main entrance was originally in Dean Bradley Street, it was as a part of Smith Square that Transport House became best known. With the HQs of the two major political parties practically next door to each other, at election time the Square was the scene of joyous triumph, as well as defeat and dejection.

The TUC moved to a new HQ in 1957, the Labour Party did likewise in 1980. The building's history as Transport House ended just before the millennium when the TGWU moved out. The Local Government Association moved in, renaming it Local Government House.

3. THE BUXTON MEMORIAL DRINKING FOUNTAIN

Designed and built by Mr Charles Buxton MP in 1865, it commemorates the struggle by Members of Parliament for the abolition of the slave trade.

4. LORD NORTH STREET

A small street with a lively political history. Virtually every house has a political connection, although, contrary to popular belief, the street has nothing to do with Lord North, the Tory Prime Minister of the 1770s and 1780s. Until 1936, it was simply North Street, but was renamed to distinguish it from other streets of the same name.

It has been popular with Conservatives, as Alan Clark noted in his diary in 1983: "I remember thinking these houses were a bit poky, blackly crumbling .. I see now, of course, that they are the choicest thing you can have if you are a Tory MP". Anthony Eden lived at no.2 in 1924; Sir Edward du Cann at no. 5 from 1965 to 1970 and no. 19 from 1970 to 1978; Brendan Bracken (1931-58) and, more recently, Sir Nigel Fisher lived at no. 10; Lord Dilhorne at no. 11, and Teresa Gorman at no. 14. No. 8 has been a hotbed of activity. During Bracken's residency in the 1930s many of the Party's anti-appeasers rallied round Churchill there, and when Jonathan Aitken lived there his home was the venue for meetings of the Conservative Philosophy Group, with speakers such as Margaret Thatcher and Richard Nixon.

The most famous non-Conservative resident was the Labour PM, Harold Wilson, who lived for at no.5 for six years. He moved there after his election defeat in 1970 and left after his surprise resignation as Prime Minister in 1976.

5. 4 COWLEY STREET

In the 1980s the Social Democratic Party was based here. Following the SDP's merger with the Liberal Party in 1988, it became the HQ of the Liberal Democrats.

6. COLLEGE GREEN

This area of grass across from the Houses of Parliament has become famous as the place for TV interviews with MPs and ministers. It came to the forefront of the public's mind during the high drama of the Conservative Party leadership election in November 1990, which led to the toppling of Margaret Thatcher in favour of John Major.

7. JEWEL TOWER

Built in the 14th century, it was for over two centuries from 1621 the Parliament Office, housing Parliament's records. After

70 years as a part of the Weights and Measures Office, it underwent major renovation work, and now hosts a fascinating public exhibition on the history and role of Parliament.

8. CHURCH HOUSE, DEAN'S YARD

Having survived a serious air raid in October 1940, Church House was seen as a possible alternative venue for Parliament to meet. Parliament met there during three stages of the War, in late 1940 (from 7 November, with the new session opened by the King on the 21st); spring 1941 (caused by the direct hit on the Commons on 10-11 May) and summer 1944. The Commons met in the Hoare Memorial Hall (a plaque marking this was unveiled by Attlee and Churchill on 28 April 1948), and the Lords in the Convocation Hall. Church House, jokingly known as the 'Churchill Club' during these periods, was the scene of many dramatic wartime parliamentary occasions.

At the end of the War it was the site of various United Nations commissions. The War Crimes Commission met in June 1945, and the preparatory commissions of the UN itself met there in late 1945. The Security Council met in Bishop Partridge Hall in January 1946. These events are commemorated in a stone in the Entrance Porch, unveiled by the then UN Secretary General, Pérez de Cuellar, in 1986.

Because of its location, Church House remained a venue for political and state meetings of all kinds. Two prime ministers of the 1950s, Anthony Eden and Harold Macmillan, were formally elected as party leader by Conservative MPs there, in April 1955 and January 1957 respectively. Many high-profile public inquiries and tribunals have been held there, such as the Bank Rate Leak Tribunal in 1957 and the Scarman Inquiry into the 1981 Brixton riots. Prime Minister Tony Blair met his huge

Parliamentary Labour Party there following his landslide general election victory in May 1997.

9. WESTMINSTER SCHOOL

This school off Dean's Yard has had many famous political pupils, including some future prime ministers - Henry Pelham, the Duke of Newcastle, the Marquess of Rockingham, the Duke of Portland and Lord John Russell.

St James's

Tucked between seats of government and monarchy, with St James's Square at its centre, this small rectangle of central London was, and to some extent remains, the heart of political society and clubland.

1. ST JAMES'S SQUARE

No. 4 was Nancy Astor's home, the first woman to sit in the House of Commons. No. 10 was, appropriately, home to three prime ministers, Chatham, Derby and Gladstone (commemorated by a plaque). As Chatham House (joined with no. 9), it is the office of the Royal Institute of International Affairs. From no. 31, Eisenhower directed the Allied Invasion of Europe in 1944. Lord Derby lived for the last fifteen years of his life at no. 33.

The Square has other Prime Ministerial connections: Walpole lived there during his premiership, and his little-known successor, the Earl of Wilmington, died there. The Duke of Grafton was married at no. 13 in 1756, and Lord Grenville lived at no. 17.

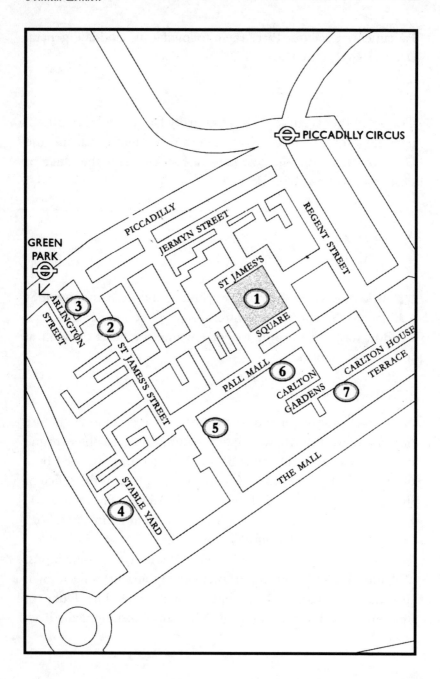

One notorious episode in the 1980s took place outside the then Libyan Embassy, the fatal shooting of PC Yvonne Fletcher during disturbances on 17 April 1984.

2. ST JAMES'S STREET

This street still houses many political clubs. It began with establishments such as White's Chocolate House, a gambling den and Tory club, established in 1693, and the Cocoa Tree Tavern, a Tory chocolate house in 1698.

Boodle's, at no. 28, was established in Pall Mall in 1762 as a political club of Lord Shelburne's supporters, but the political connection soon lapsed. White's, at no. 37, had many notable political members, including lots of prime ministers, but became primarily non-political after the formation of the Carlton Club in 1832. Charles James Fox lived in the street, and was a member of Brooks's (no.60). When his debts threatened to overwhelm him, he was rescued by some of his fellow members.

Probably the best known of the clubs is the Carlton, the main Tory establishment. It grew out of unofficial attempts at party organisation by the 'Charles Street Gang', operating out of the home of the Mayfair home of Joseph Planta. It gained political immortality when it was the venue of the meeting of Tory MPs in October 1922 which led to the removal of the Lloyd George coalition government, to be replaced by a Conservative administration under Bonar Law. This meeting was the genesis of the Conservative backbench parliamentary '1922 Committee'.

3. ARLINGTON STREET

This small street has played host to many political figures. Britain's first prime minister, Sir Robert Walpole, who lived at no. 17 from 1716 to 1731, died in 1745 at no.5 (marked by a

GLC plaque). A plaque at no. 9 records that Charles James Fox lived there from 1804-6. Others who lived in the street included the Salisburys, and the 18th century politicians, Lord Carteret and William Pulteney.

No.22 was built in 1743 for long-time PM of the mid-18th century, Henry Pelham, who died there in 1754. The house was later known as Hamilton House and, from 1880, as Wimborne House. In 1926 it was the scene of talks between the coal owners and trade union leaders which led to the ending of the General Strike.

4. LANCASTER HOUSE

This was formerly known as Godolphin House (where Charles James Fox lived shortly before his death), York House (when occupied by the Duke of York) and Stafford House (where the social reformer Shaftesbury and William Garrison, the US slavery abolitionist spoke). It became Lancaster House in 1913 and was given to the nation the following year. It is frequently used for major state and diplomatic occasions. Churchill as PM hosted a banquet for the Queen shortly after her coronation in 1953, and Edward Heath announced Stage II of his government's prices & incomes policy at a press conference here in January 1973. It was also the site of major conferences on Kenya in the early 1960s; Rhodesia/Zimbabwe (1979-80); Bosnia (July and December 1995); Nazi gold in December 1997, and on humanitarian aid to Iraq in April 1998.

5. MARLBOROUGH HOUSE

This was the 'court' of the Prince of Wales after the death of Prince Albert in the late 19th century. It was the site of Marlborough House Balls, especially the fancy dress ball on 22

July 1874, which saw the Prince dressed as Charles I. Gladstone was allowed to appear in uniform instead of fancy dress after he had been dining and speaking at Mansion House. It now houses the Commonwealth Secretariat.

6. PALL MALL

Like St James's Street, home to many clubs. One of the more famous was the Reform at no. 104, which began in 1836 as a meeting place for radicals, and was long associated with leading Liberal politicians from Gladstone and Palmerston in the 19th century, to Lloyd George and Churchill in the 20th. Sir Henry Campbell-Bannerman was elected Liberal leader there in 1899. Other clubs include the Travellers' at no. 106 (from which Lord Rosebery and Lord Randolph Churchill were blackballed), and the Athenaeum at no. 107.

7. THE CARLTONS

Carlton Gardens and Carlton House Terrace are rich in political connections. Gladstone lived in nos. 13 (1839-48) and 11 (1856-75) Carlton House Terrace, broken by 8 years at 6 Carlton Gardens (1848-56).

No. 1 Carlton Gardens was also the residence of Viscount Goderich (the Tory PM) and, when in exile, Louis Napoleon. It is the official residence of the Foreign Secretary. No. 3 was said to be the base for MI6's recruitment. No 4 was home to two prime ministers, Balfour and Palmerston, the latter noted by a plaque. De Gaulle lived there from 1940 to 1943, when it was the HQ of Free French forces. There is a Cross of Lorraine memorial and statue of de Gaulle nearby. Margaret and Denis Thatcher had their wedding reception on 13 December 1951 at no. 5.

Lord Curzon lived at one Carlton House Terrace, and died there, and there is a statue of him opposite at the corner of Carlton Gardens. The Conservative PM, Lord Derby, lived at no. 11 (there is a plaque, shared with Gladstone).

Berkeley Square

Not surprisingly, such a fashionable square has been home to many political leaders over the decades.

1. BERKELEY SQUARE

Lord Rosebery lived at no. 2 and at no. 38 (the latter is now Berger House); Lewis Harcourt at no. 14 and Pitt the Younger at no. 47 (now HSBC Bank). The latter belonged to Pitt's elder brother, John, 2nd Earl of Chatham. Earl Grey lived at no. 48 (now the ScotiaBank), which he rented out between 1830 and 1834 to Henry, Lord Brougham, the Lord Chancellor, who apparently left the house in a terrible mess. Canning lived at no. 50 (said to be the haunted house of the Square) in 1806-7, marked by a GLC plaque.

2. BRUTON STREET

George Canning lived at no. 24. At no. 17, across the road on the south side, on 21 April 1926 the present Queen Elizabeth II was born. There is a private plaque to mark this event.

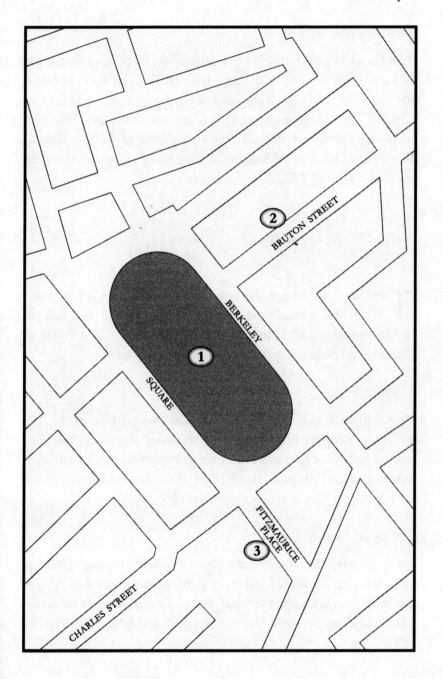

3. LANSDOWNE HOUSE

The Lansdowne Club at no. 9 Fitzmaurice Place is all that is left of Lansdowne House, which was built in 1761 by Robert Adam for the Earl of Bute. Bute sold the property for £22,500 to another PM, Shelburne, who took up residence in 1768. The treaty of American Independence was drafted in the Round Room in 1783. Harold Macmillan's wedding reception was held here on 21 April 1920.

Grosvenor Square

This Square has been the American heart of London since the 1780s. Its transatlantic connections earned it the title of 'Little America', and during the last War, it was known as 'Eisenhowerplatz'.

1. THE UNITED STATES EMBASSY

The Square is dominated by the monumental pile of the US Embassy, with its huge eagle, on the west side. The Embassy moved here in 1938, and the modern edifice (much of which is actually below ground) dates from 1960. It was the focus for anti-Vietnam War demonstrations in 1968.

2. GROSVENOR SQUARE

John Adams (2nd president) lived at no. 9, in the 1780s. A commemorative plaque states, in part: 'John Adams and Abigail his wife through character and personality did much to create understanding between the two English-speaking countries. In

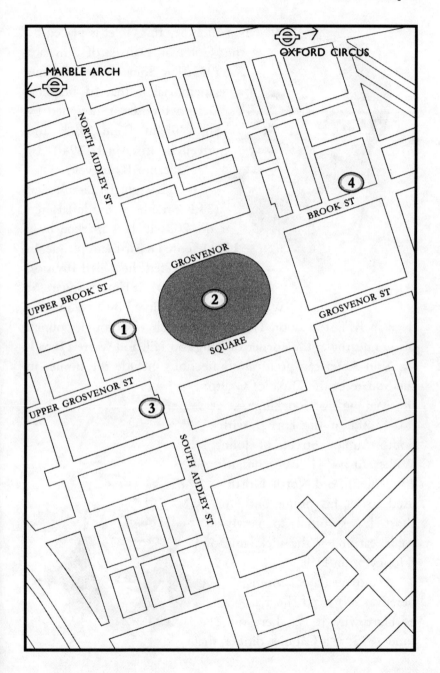

their memory this tablet is placed by the Colonial Dames of America 1933.' The Square's most famous memorial is that to Franklin Delano Roosevelt, designed by Sir William Reid Dick and unveiled in April 1948 by Eleanor Roosevelt.

Dwight D. Eisenhower (34th president) headquartered at no. 20, which is marked by a US Defense Department plaque. In 1944 he directed the Allied Invasion of Europe from 31 St James's Square, St James's SW1, which is also marked by a plaque. Ike lived in Kingston upon Thames, marked by a borough council plaque nearby at the corner of Kingston Hill and Warren Road.

Non-American political connections include the homes in the Square of the Duke of Grafton, the Marquess of Rockingham at no. 4, and, at the corner with South Audley Street, of John Wilkes. At no. 41, lived (and, in 1792, died) Lord North. North used to let his house out on short leases, often to newly-weds, earning it the nickname of 'Honeymoon Hall'.

At no. 39 (later renumbered as 44) lived the Earl of Harrowby. It was here on 21 June 1815, at a Cabinet dinner, that the first news arrived of Wellington's victory over Napoleon at Waterloo. The house was known thereafter as 'Waterloo House', and was, five years later, intended to be the site of the assassination of the Cabinet at another dinner, by the Cato Street conspirators (see *Plots*).

3. SOUTH AUDLEY STREET

Lord John Russell lived at no. 66, and the Earl of Bute died at Bute House, no. 75. Palmerston lived on the other side of the Square, in North Audley Street.

4. BROOK STREET

William Pitt, Earl of Chatham, lived at no. 68. At no. 43 was a Conservative club, the Bath Club. It began in Dover Street in 1894, moved to new premises in St James's Street after the original site burned down during the Second World War, and merged with the Conservative Club in 1950. The club moved to Brook Street in 1959, though the site now houses a private bank. On the other side of the Square its sister street, Upper Brook Street, was the home of Baldwin and of George Grenville.

Hanover Square

Like Berkeley Square, Hanover Square was a fashionable centre for the political elite, especially the prime ministers of the 18th and 19th centuries.

1. HANOVER SQUARE

Palmerston owned property here, Earl Grey lived in the Square and Lord Grenville married Anne Pitt, daughter of Lord

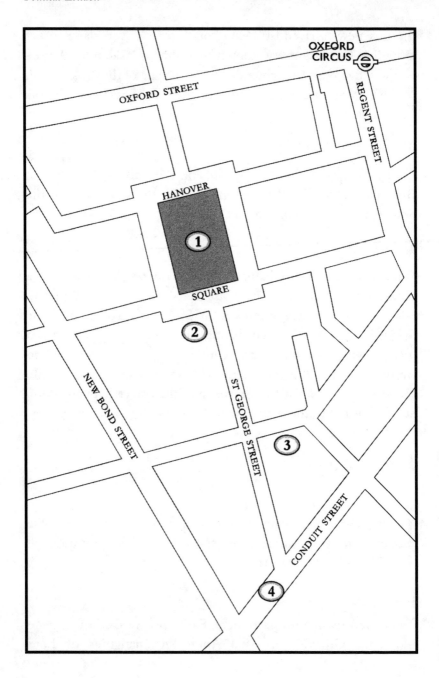

Camelford, here in 1792. One of the Marquess of Rockingham's close political allies, the Yorkshire MP Sir George Savile, lived in what was described as 'one of the most expensive houses' in the Square from 1755 to 1764. Talleyrand lived at no. 21 in the 1830s. At the south end of the Square is the large bronze statue of William Pitt the Younger, by Sir Francis Legatt Chantrey. It was erected in 1831, and survived attempts by Reform Bill supporters to pull it down on its unveiling day.

2. ST GEORGE STREET

Known as George Street until 1938, two Lord Chancellors, Cowper and Lyndhurst, lived here, as did RB Sheridan, who was an MP as well as a noted dramatist. Disraeli lived for a time at Edward's Hotel.

3. ST GEORGE'S CHURCH

This famous church has seen many political marriages, including those of Castlereagh (1794); Addington (1823); Grey (1805); Russell (1835); Palmerston (1839); Disraeli (1839) and Asquith (1894). When Asquith married Margot Tennant on 10 May 1894, four Premiers signed the register – Gladstone, Rosebery, Balfour, Asquith – and a fifth, Campbell-Bannerman, was in the congregation. Asquith lived at 20 Cavendish Square for a time, just across Oxford Street from Hanover Square.

4. CONDUIT STREET

Charles James Fox was born here in January 1749. George Canning lived at no. 37, and Lord Liverpool also lived in the Street.

Also in and around London

There are many other areas of London which are mini–Hot Spots in their own right, and well worth exploring. Many are covered in the following sections of this book within their particular themes. Here are some of the more interesting:

BELGRAVIA

This large sweep of SW1 contains several hot spots, primarily clustered around Eaton and Belgrave Squares, belying Disraeli's caustic comment that 'The Belgrave District is as monotonous as Marylebone, and is so contrived as to be at the same time insipid and tawdry'. In Eaton Square itself, lived such diverse characters as Metternich (at no. 44, in 1848, where Wellington was a frequent caller), Lord John Russell (at no. 48, in 1858), Stanley Baldwin (at no. 93, from 1913 to 1923), Lord Halifax, who lost to Churchill in the battle to succeed Chamberlain as PM in May 1940 (at no. 86) and the flamboyant Tory MP, Bob Boothby (at no. 1, from 1946 to 1986).

In adjacent Eaton Place, lived Sir Edward Carson (at no. 5), Sir John Lubbock, first Baron Avebury, promoter of the Bank Holidays Act 1871 (at no. 29). At no. 16 lived the MP William Ewart, the Victorian MP who was not only responsible for the first Public Libraries Act in 1850, but, by being the first advocate of a scheme to commemorate the houses of the famous in London, was invaluable in identifying the political sites of the capital for future generations, such as readers of this book.

South of Eaton Square lies South Eaton Place home to luminaries such as Robert Cecil, Viscount Cecil of Chelwood, a founder of the League of Nations (at no 16, from 1923 to 1958), the noted peace campaigner, Philip Noel Baker, and the controversial Conservative MP, Enoch Powell.

To the north, before reaching Hyde Park, is the Belgrave Square area. A landmark is the monument to Simon Bolivar, unveiled in 1974 by James Callaghan, then Foreign Secretary, in the south-east corner of the Square, opposite Upper Belgrave Street. An influential diarist, Henry 'Chips' Channon, held court at no. 5 from 1935 until his death in 1958. His entry for the first of February 1943 characteristically claimed that '5 Belgrave Square has played a considerable role in politics and society, and since the war has been, if it was not already so before, the centre of London ... no true chronicler of the time could fail to record its glories and its influence.' Walter Bagehot, editor of the *Economist* and a hugely influential writer on the British constitution, lived at 12 Upper Belgrave Street from 1860 to 1877.

Thames Riverside

South of the Palace of Westminster the riverside area is full of political interest, especially in Millbank. At no. 4 is a media centre from which TV and radio companies broadcast their coverage of political and parliamentary affairs. You can often see famous politicians going to and from interviews. 7 Millbank is currently used as Parliamentary offices, and many government and public bodies are based in the area. Further down the road, just past Lambeth Bridge, is Thames House, an anonymous looking building which is the HQ of MI5. Just across the river at Vauxhall Cross, conveniently, the ostentatious yellow and green building is the headquarters of MI6. Also on Millbank is Millbank Tower, where the Labour Party has its head office.

Beyond Pimlico is the Chelsea Embankment, where there is a statue of Sir Thomas More. The noted Victorian Liberal politician, George Robinson, Marquess of Ripon lived at no. 9. The Chelsea Hospital, in adjacent Royal Hospital Road, has several prime ministerial connections. Wellington lay in state there in the Great Hall in 1852, ironically 44 years after facing a humiliating court of enquiry at the same site following the infamous Convention of Cintra during the Peninsular War. The Earl of Wilmington, Walpole's successor, was a Treasurer of the Hospital and the Earl of Bute was a Commissioner. Carrying on west along the Chelsea riverside, Cheyne Walk has been home to many notables, such as Sylvia Pankhurst, Lloyd George and, more recently, the Tory minister, Paul Channon. In adjacent Cheyne Row was no. 5, the residence of Thomas Carlyle, the 'Sage of Chelsea'.

BLOOMSBURY

Bloomsbury Square has a statue of Charles James Fox, and no. 6 was the home of Isaac D'Israeli and his more famous son. 140 Gower Street was a former HQ of MI5. The Georgian PM, Shelburne, was married in 1779 at St George's, Bloomsbury Way. The suffragist, Lady Jane Strachey, died in 1928 in Gordon Square.

COVENT GARDEN

King Street became noted as the site of the HQ of the Communist Party, and, at no. 38, is the Africa Centre, opened by President Kaunda of Zambia in November 1964. At 40 Maiden Lane lived Andrew Marvell, who was not only a literary figure, but was also MP for Hull. Georgiana, Duchess of Devonshire, took lodgings in Henrietta Street when campaigning for Fox during the famous 1784 Westminster election. There was a noted rally against Irish Home Rule at the Royal Opera House, Floral Street, on 16 May 1886.

THE CITY

Being the ancient heart of London, the 'square mile' and its environs have a long and varied political history. There are many sites connected with the Lord Mayor, Richard Whittington, of pantomime fame. He lived on a house on the site of 19 College Hill, and founded and was buried in St Michael Paternoster Royal Church in that street. Sir Francis Walsingham, Elizabeth I's minister, died in Seething Lane, off Great Tower Street in 1590. Wellington and Peel were original members of the City of London Club at 19 Old Broad Street. In Salisbury Square there is a memorial to Robert Waithman MP, a Lord Mayor and supporter of parliamentary reform, erected in 1833. Oliver Cromwell was married at St Giles, Cripplegate in 1620. Disraeli was articled to a firm of solicitors, Swains in 1821-24 at 6 Frederick's Place, Old Jewry, and Asquith was educated at the City of London School, Milk Street, off Cheapside. Fleet Street was not only synonymous with the print media, it also has a bronze bust of the Parnellite MP and journalist, TP O'Connor, and at no. 69 there is a plaque to John Bright and Richard Cobden, leading lights in the Anti-Corn Law League in the 1840s, which was based here.

EAST END

Sidney Street E1 was the site of a famous police siege of anarchists in January 1911. The celebrated 1888 'match-girls' strike' took place at the Bryant & May factory in Fairfield Road, Bow (marked by a plaque at the Fairfield Works). Attlee lived at Commercial Road, Limehouse, and in residences at two East London social organisations, Haileybury House, Durham Road, Stepney and Toynbee Hall in Whitechapel. The local and national Labour leader, George Lansbury, lived in a house on the site of

39 Bow Road E3 for 23 years, and the long-time Labour politician, Manny Shinwell, was born in 1884 at Brune House, Toynbee Street, Spitalfields. In Bow Churchyard, Bow Road, there is a bronze statue of Gladstone, by Albert Bruce-Joy, 1882, a gift of Theodore Bryant (of match company), to commemorate WEG's 50 years as an MP.

HAMPSTEAD

The area of north-west London in and around Hampstead has long associations with the left/progressive end of politics (hence the term 'Hampstead liberal'). It was home to Labour leaders such as Ramsay MacDonald (9 Howitt Road, Belsize Park, and then 103 Frognal), Hugh Gaitskell (18 Frognal Gardens), Harold Wilson (10 and 12 Southway, Hampstead Garden Suburb) and Michael Foot (Pilgrim's Lane). Beatrice and Sidney Webb lived at 10 Fitzjohn's Avenue and briefly at 10 Netherall Gardens, and George Orwell lived at 77 Parliament Hill in 1945, and worked at Westrope's Bookshop (on the site of the later Prompt Corner Café), South End Green in 1934. Asquith lived in Eton House, John Street (now Keats Grove), and at 4 Maresfield Gardens. The unfortunate Spencer Perceval lived at Belsize House, and Perceval Avenue is named after him. Parliament Hill is said to be so called because of the legend that Guy Fawkes and his co-plotters planned to watch the explosion of the Houses of Parliament from there. The notorious Kit Cat Club met at the Upper Flask Tavern, off East Heath Road.

POLITICAL
LANDSCAPES

Plots

The dark streets and alleyways of London have been home to innumerable plots, and conspirators have come from far and wide to undermine the political status quo.

Spa Fields to Cato Street

The early 19th century was a period of domestic unrest in London. A mass meeting was organised for Spa Fields, Clerkenwell, EC1 on 2 December 1816. Henry 'Orator' Hunt spoke to a large crowd at the nearby Merlin's Cave Tavern. When the authorities dispersed the crowd, some of the demonstrators tried to march on the City.

One Spa Fields organiser, Arthur Thistlewood, pursued more militant means. On 22 February 1820 he was told of a planned Cabinet dinner the following evening at the home of the Lord President of the Council, the Earl of Harrowby at no. 39 (later 44) Grosvenor Square, W1. He planned to murder them, and topple the government. A scheme was quickly concocted with fellow conspirators in a hayloft over a stable at no. 6 (later 1a) Cato Street, W1. Two sacks were brought to carry off the heads of two senior ministers, Lords Sidmouth (the former PM, Addington) and Castlereagh, to be displayed on pikes on the steps of the Mansion House, EC4. When the authorities heard of the plot, they sent police and soldiers into Cato Street on the 23rd. The loft was stormed and most of the conspirators captured, but Thistlewood killed one of the police officers and fled. He was caught at no. 8 White Street, Little Moorfields. The conspirators were imprisoned in the Tower of London, Thistlewood himself in the Bloody Tower. Five of them including Thistlewood, were hanged outside Newgate Prison, EC4 (the site is now the Old Bailey) on 1 May.

London has been the scene of other revolutionary schemes, the most famous was the Gunpowder Plot, by a group which included Guy Fawkes. This was an attempt to blow up Parliament and the King on 5 November 1605. The plot was discovered, as is recorded in a plaque at 244-278 Crondall Street, Hoxton N1: 'In a house near this site on the 12th October 1605 Lord Monteagle received a letter unmasking the plot led by Guy Fawkes to blow up the Houses of Parliament'. Fawkes and the others were tried in Westminster Hall and executed on 1 February 1606 in Old Palace Yard, Westminster SW1.

More recently, the Conservative Cabinet was the target of an IRA mortar attack on No. 10 Downing Street on 7 February 1991, during the Gulf War. No one was injured. The Prime Minister, John Major, said, 'I think we'd better start again somewhere else' and the meeting adjourned to the secure 'Cobra Room' underground. The mortars were fired from a van parked at the corner of Horse Guards Avenue, next to the Banqueting House.

SMOKE-FILLED ROOMS

Political history is full of party leadership plots. For example, just two days after the sudden death of Labour Party leader, Hugh Gaitskell in January 1963, Tony Crosland's top-floor flat in the Boltons, Chealsea SW10, was the scene of a meeting of those in the party determined to stop Harold Wilson from winning the leadership election. Further meetings took place in the flat of Jack Diamond in Greycoat Place, Westminster, SW1. There was a similar meeting took place in the house of the Tory junior minister, Tristan Garel-Jones at 12 Catherine Place, Westminster,

SW1 following the failure of Margaret Thatcher to win re-election as party leader on the first ballot in November 1990.

At the height of the Tory leadership election in the summer of 1995, journalists spotted BT engineers outside 11 Lord North Street, SW1, apparently installing new telephone and fax lines, and several Tory notables were seen entering the house. The rumour immediately spread that the house was being prepared for a leadership bid by the cabinet minister, Michael Portillo, which he refused to confirm or deny at the time.

Political Women

From the suffragettes onwards London has been a centre of feminist movements and radical women have left their mark on London's landscape.

SUFFRAGETTES

A notable example of women's political activity in modern times is perhaps the suffragist (or suffragette) movement, and there are plenty of relevant sites in central London.

The headquarters of the Women's Social and Political Union, founded by Emmeline Pankhurst, were at no. 4 Clement's Inn, off the Aldwych, WC2, in 1907. There is a memorial to the suffrage movement in the north-west corner of Christchurch Gardens, Victoria Street, SW1, known as the Suffragette Scroll (1970), which has a stirring inscription.

Some sites reflecting suffragist action are 10 Downing Street, SW1 itself, where three activists tried to disrupt a Cabinet meeting in January 1908, two of them by chaining themselves to the railings. Following a similar incident in March 1912, when stones were thrown at the windows of No. 10, some demonstrators were arrested and held at the former police station in nearby Cannon Row (now Canon Row) SW1.

In a cupboard in the Crypt Chapel under Westminster Hall, Emily Wilding Davison, hid for 48 hours in 1911 so that she could put 'House of Commons' as her address in that year's census. In 1989–90 Tony Benn erected a plaque in the small room to mark her protest against the then Liberal Government's failure to legislate for women's suffrage. Davison later became the movement's most famous martyr when she fatally threw herself under the King's horse during the Epsom Derby in 1913.

Leaders of the WSPU were the Pankhursts, Emmeline and her daughters, Christabel and Sylvia. Sylvia lived at 120 Cheyne Walk, Chelsea, SW10 and at nearby 45 Park Walk. She set up an East London toy factory and babies' nursery at 45 Norman Grove, E3, marked by a plaque. Emmeline is buried at Brompton Cemetery, Old Brompton Road, West Brompton SW6. There is an impressive memorial to her, and to Christabel, in the Victoria Tower Gardens, Millbank, SW1, which was unveiled by Stanley Baldwin in 1930.

Caxton Hall, Caxton Street, SW1 was a well-known venue for many suffrage meetings (the Suffragette Scroll is only yards away), including one organised by the Pankhursts in February 1906, on the day of the State Opening of Parliament. When they heard that the King's Speech did not contain any promise of women's suffrage, they marched on Parliament in protest.

Hyde Park was the scene of a huge meeting of 50,000, on 26 July 1913, marking the culmination of a six week Women's Pilgrimage. Also in Hyde Park is the Reformer's Tree, a spot (nowadays marked by a lamp post) where an oak tree once grew, which was a rallying point for the Reform League and other protest groups, and weekly meetings of the WSPU were held near it.

LEADING FEMINISTS

Dame Millicent Fawcett, president of the National Union of Women's Suffrage Societies from 1897 to 1919, and an opponent of the Pankhursts' more militant approach, lived at 2 Gower Street, Bloomsbury, WC1 (where there is an LCC plaque), where she died in 1929. There is a memorial to her in Westminster Abbey.

Three residences of Mary Wollstonecraft, a key feminist writer of the late 18th century, are at 209-215 Blackfriars Road, Southwark, SE1; 373 Mare Street, Hackney, E8, and Oakshott Court, Werrington Street, Somers Town, NW1. She was originally buried in Old St Pancras Churchyard, NW1, where her headstone remains.

PARTY POLITICALS

Countess Constance Markievicz was interned in Holloway Prison for almost a year in 1918 to 1919. During this time she became the first woman to be elected to the House of Commons, as a Sinn Fein MP for Dublin, but she refused to take her seat. So the honour of the first woman to sit in Parliament (as a Conservative in 1919) went to Nancy Astor. Lady Astor was married in All Souls Church, Langham Place, Marylebone, W1 on 3 May 1906, and lived at Astor House, 2 Temple Place, WC2, and at 4 St James's Square, SW1, where there is a plaque.

Margaret MacDonald, the wife of the first Labour Prime Minister, Ramsay MacDonald, was an active social and political reformer. She was born at 17 Pembridge Square, Bayswater, W2 and died at her home at 3 Lincoln's Inn Fields, Covent Garden, WC2 in September 1911 when she was only 41. There is a bronze memorial seat to her on the north side of the Fields, by R R Goulden, which was unveiled in December 1914. It shows her surrounded by nine children, and the inscription records that she "spent her life in helping others."

The socialist writer Vera Brittain (mother of Shirley Williams) is commemorated by plaques at two addresses, 11 Wymering Mansions, Wymering Road, Maida Vale, W9 and 58 Doughty Street, off Gray's Inn Road, WC1.

Britain's first woman Prime Minister, Margaret Thatcher, has lived in a number of London addresses, including Swan Court, Chelsea; Eaton Square, Belgravia; Westminster Gardens, Marsham Street, SW1, and St George's Square Mews, Pimlico. She married Denis Thatcher at Wesley's Chapel, City Road, EC1 on 13 December 1951. The office of the Margaret Thatcher Foundation is at 76 Chesham Place, Belgravia.

Strangers in a Strange Land

It is not surprising that such a major capital city has been home to many notable people from abroad. Some have come as refugees or exiles, perhaps from domestic oppression, or imigrants in search of a way out of poverty. Some of these people's London sojourns are marked by plaques, statues and other memorials.

BENJAMIN FRANKLIN

Franklin left his mark across political and social London. He lived for many years at 7 (now 36)

Craven Street, off Charing Cross WC2, lodging with son, William, in the house of a Mrs Stephenson. It nearly burned down in 1762, as he recorded: 'Our house and yard were covered with falling coals of fire, but, as it rained hard, nothing catched' (LCC plaque). He worked in the printing shop in the Lady Chapel of St Bartholomew the Great, St Bartholomew Close, Smithfield, EC1 in 1724.

MAHATMA GANDHI

A leader of non-violent Indian nationalism, he spent his first night in London in 1881 at the Victoria Hotel, Northumberland Avenue, WC2, and lived at 20 Baron's Court Road, Hammersmith, W14, while a law student at the Inner Temple. He also lived in Kingsley Hall, 21 Powis Road, E3, a centre for the poor of the East End. Tavistock Square, WC1 has a statue of Gandhi at its centre, unveiled by Harold Wilson in 1968.

MOHAMMED JINNAH

A founder of Pakistan, he was a law student at Lincoln's Inn. He lived at 35 Russell Road, W14 in 1895, marked by an LCC plaque, and bought a house in West Heath Road, Hampstead, NW3.

GIUSEPPE MAZZINI

A leading Italian nationalist, he lived at 183 North Gower Street, Bloomsbury, NW1 (1837-40), and studied at the British Museum. He also lived for a number of years at 18 Fulham Road, SW6. There are two other plaques in central London honouring him as an apostle of Italian democracy. Both were erected privately. One is at 5 Hatton Garden, EC1, and the other at 10 Laystall Street, EC1, where he founded the Italian Operatives' Society in defence of Italian workers. It became the Mazzini and Garibaldi Club, later based at 51 Red Lion Street, EC1.

KARL MARX

His first London house was 4 Anderson Street, Chelsea SW3, from which the family were evicted for non-payment of rent. They moved to the German Hotel, 1 Leicester Street, WC2 (later the site of Manzi's, a fish restaurant), and then for six years in nearby Dean Street, Soho, W1. Six months were spent at no. 64, and from 1850-56 in two rooms on the top floor at no.28, above the later Leoni's Quo Vadis Restaurant.

The choice of the latter residence as the site of a blue plaque was not uncontroversial. Peppino Leoni, the downstairs restaurateur, was outraged: 'My clientele is the very best ... rich people .. nobility and royalty — and Marx was the person who wanted to get rid of them all!'. Nevertheless, a GLC plaque was erected there. It is not known what effect it had on the local economy.

The family then spent eight years at no. 9 (later no. 46) Grafton Terrace, Gospel Oak, NW1, and then in nearby Maitland

Park Road. They lived first at no. 1 (then 1 Modena Villas) and, later, for the last eight years of Marx's life, at no. 41 (rebuilt, after being bombed in the last war, as nos. 101–108).

Among the many sites in central London connected with Marx and his circle are 18 Greek Street, Soho, W1, the first meeting place of the International Working Men's Association, and St Martin's Hall, Long Acre, Covent Garden, WC2, site of the First International in September 1864. The Marx Memorial Library is at Marx House, Clerkenwell Green, EC1.

Marx was buried in Highgate Cemetery, Swain's Lane, N6 in March 1883, and was later moved to the present site in the East Cemetery in 1954. The famous massive bronze bust of Marx was placed there in 1956. Other members of the Marx family are also buried there.

VLADIMIR ILICH LENIN

Soviet Communist revolutionary leader, he lived at 16 Percy Circus, south of Pentonville Road, WC1 in 1905, marked by a private plaque on the site of the property. He also lived in a number of places around London, including 30 Holford Square (off King's Cross Road/Great Percy Street) in 1903, a monument opposite unveiled by the Soviet ambassador 1943, and 6 Oakley Square, Camden Town NW1 in 1911.

He pursued his radical political activities in London. In what became the Marx Memorial Library, Marx House, Clerkenwell Green, EC1 was the first office of Twentieth Century Press which printed 17 issues of Iskra (The Spark). The Jewish Social Club Hall in Fulbourne Street, E1 held the 5th Congress of the Russian Social Democratic Labour Party, attended by luminaries such as Lenin, Stalin and Trotsky.

LOUIS NAPOLEON

The future Napoleon III, nephew of Bonaparte and Emperor of France, lived in London over several periods. Among his residences in fashionable St James's, SW1 were 1c King Street, 1 Carlton Gardens, and the Brunswick Hotel, Jermyn Street, (where he adopted the alias of the Comte d'Arenberg). Following his defeat in the Franco-Prussian war in 1870, he returned to Britain, living outside urban London in Camden Place, Chislehurst Common, Chislehurst. He enjoyed London living, being an honorary member of the Army and Navy Club, and a habitué of Crockford's. When he returned as Emperor, and was processing up St James's Street, he was spotted pointing out to his wife 'with interest and pleasure' his former home at 1c King Street.

Others who have spent some time in London include:

JAWAHARLAL NEHRU

India's first Prime Minister lived at 60 Elgin Crescent, W11 from 1910 until 1912 while he was a student at the Inner Temple.

THOMAS MASARYK

Future Czechoslovak president, lived and worked at 21 Platt's Lane, NW3 during World War I.

SIMON BOLIVAR

Latin American nationalist leader, lived at 4 Duke Street, W1 in 1810. A monument to him in Belgrave Square, SW1, was unveiled by James Callaghan (then Foreign Secretary) in 1974.

EDWARD BENES

Czech leader, lived at 28 Gwendolen Avenue, off Upper Richmond Road, Putney, SW15.

FRANCISCO DE MIRANDA

South American nationalist leader, lived at 58 Grafton Way, W1 (1803-10). There is also a statue in adjoining Fitzroy Street.

DAVID BEN GURION

Israeli premier, lived at 75 Warrington Crescent, Maida Vale, W9.

SLOBODAN YOVANOVITCH

Prime Minister of Yugoslavia, lived at 58-66 Cromwell Road, South Kensington, SW7 from 1945 to 1958

LAJOS (LOUIS) KOSSUTH

Hungarian mid-19th century nationalist, lived at 39 Chepstow Villas, Notting Hill, W11.

MARCUS GARVEY

Black nationalist, lived briefly at 2 Beaumont Crescent, Earl's Court, W14.

RAMMOHAN ROY

First ambassador to Britain of the Mogul Emperor, lived at 29 Bedford Square, WC1.

SUN YAT SEN

Chinese revolutionary leader, lived at 4 Warwick Court, Gray's Inn, WC1, and at 49 Portland Place, W1, in 1896.

BERNARDO O'HIGGINS

Chilean nationalist leader, lived at Clarence House, 2 The Vineyard, Richmond.

Riots & Affrays

As Britain's centre of government, London has attracted more than its fair share of political protests, many of which have had enormous historical significance.

PEASANTS' REVOLT, JUNE 1381

A protest against economic conditions and imposition of poll taxes, it was most significant in Kent where it was led by Wat Tyler. His protesters marched on London, meeting up with other groups at Blackheath Gate, Greenwich and elsewhere. The Tower of London itself was occupied, and King Richard II was forced to negotiate with Tyler at Smithfield. However, Tyler was mortally wounded by the Lord Mayor of London, Sir William Walworth, and was carried to St Bartholomew's Hospital, Smithfield, EC1. It is said that Tyler was later dragged out of the building and beheaded. At Fishmongers Hall, London Bridge (north side) EC3, the Fishmongers' Company has the dagger reputedly used by Walworth to stab Tyler. There is a life-size wooden statue of Walworth (1684) on the main staircase.

GORDON RIOTS, JUNE 1780

A week of anti-Catholic rioting and a march on Westminster from St George's Fields, Southwark caused many deaths and injuries throughout London, following Lord George Gordon's petition against Catholic relief legislation. The homes of many leading political figures were attacked. The Prime Minister, Lord North, was threatened by a mob in Downing Street. Churches were attacked, including the Sardinian Chapel, close by Lincoln's Inn Fields, WC2, and the Bavarian Chapel in Warwick Street, Soho, W1. Prisons around London were invaded, and prisoners released; bridges were captured and even the Bank of England was under siege.

Rioters attacked the Bloomsbury home of Lord Mansfield, the Lord Chief Justice, but, on finding their quarry not there, went to his Kenwood house in Hampstead. They stopped en route at the Spaniard's Inn, Spaniard's Road, NW3, where the landlord managed to delay them with offers of drink until the military arrived and captured them.

When an inventory was taken in 1782 of the contents of the Grosvenor Square home of the Whig leader, the Marquess of Rockingham, it was found to include 'an iron bar taken from one of the rioters in June 1780'.

THE BATTLE OF CABLE STREET, OCTOBER 1936

Locals tried to prevent a march by Oswald Mosley's British Union of Fascists through an area in Whitechapel, E1, originally

Gardiner's Corner at the junction of Whitechapel Street and Leman Street. The marchers re-routed through Cable Street, passing the junction with Christian Street. Anti-fascist protesters fought with police. These events led to the passing of the Public Order Act 1936. There is a mural of the 'Battle' In St George's Town Hall, 236 Cable Street.

Scandals

L ondon has inevitably had its share of political scandals over the years. Some examples are included below:

- Gladstone's curious preoccupation with 'fallen women' in various parts of London (including Haymarket, SW1 and Great Windmill Street, W1).

- Charles Stewart Parnell's catastrophic affair with Kitty O'Shea, whom he met at a dinner party at the O'Sheas' Victoria flat in 1880, and with whom he stayed in Wonersh Lodge, Eltham, then a suburban village in south-east London.

- The affairs (at his flat at 76 Sloane Street, Belgravia, SW1) which destroyed the Cabinet career of Sir Charles Dilke, MP for Chelsea, in the mid-1880s.

- The alleged blackmailing of Ramsay MacDonald by an Austrian woman in Horseferry Road, SW1, over erotic love poetry she claimed he had sent to her.

TWO FRAUDSTERS

- Horatio Bottomley learned the tricks of his later trade as a serial swindler when he was an office boy at a solicitors' firm in Coleman Street, off Moorgate, EC2. He had a line of failed publishing ventures, leading to bankruptcy, the loss of his Pall Mall flat and the loss, after only two years, of his parliamentary seat in 1912. He became an MP again six years later, but resumed his career of financial criminality, and ended up in jail. He died in 1932, following a heart attack at the Windmill Theatre.

• J. Maundy Gregory, a key fixer in the 'honours for sale' affair during Lloyd George's premiership, lived at 10 Hyde Park Terrace, W2. He operated from a suite of offices at 38 Parliament Street, SW1, where he went to great lengths to avoid detection by varying his daily route to work, and by always using the back door onto Canon Row.

THE PROFUMO SCANDAL

This had everything, including sex and spies, and when it blew open in 1963, it hastened the demise of Harold Macmillan's premiership a few months later.

The scandal revolved around the activities and friends of an osteopath, Stephen Ward, who worked at 38 Devonshire Street W1. He lived at 17 Wimpole Mews, Marylebone, W1, where Christine Keeler (who had a flat at 63 Great Cumberland Place, Marylebone, W1) met the Soviet naval attaché, Yevgeny Ivanov and the Secretary of State for War, John Profumo (who lived at Chester Terrace, on the east side of Regent's Park, NW1) at different times. Ward had to leave his home and move to a flat at Bryanston Mews, W1, which once belonged to the notorious landlord, Peter Rachman. Various entertainment venues featured in the scandal, from the Rio Café, Westbourne Park Road, Notting Hill, W11, to an 'All Nighters Club' in Wardour Street, Soho, W1.

Two 18th Century Giants

John Wilkes was born in 1725 in St John's Square, Islington, EC1. He married an heiress, Mary Meade, in 1747 in St John's Church, St John's Square, EC1. Wilkes was an MP until 1790, and also Lord Mayor of London in 1774. Issue 45 of his journal, the *North Briton*, in April 1763, attacking the King's speech proroguing Parliament, led to prolonged legal battles with the authorities. He also fought a duel with a government supporter, Samuel Martin, in November 1763 in Hyde Park, receiving a serious bullet wound in the stomach.

He had many addresses throughout central London, including 13 Great George Street, SW1 until 1764; 7 Princess Court, Westminster until 1790; St James's Place, SW1, and 30 Grosvenor Square, W1. He also resided at 2 Kensington Gore, SW7, where he set up his lover and their daughter. The Tower of London was also his 'residence' for a time in 1763, as was the King's Bench Prison, near St George's Fields, Southwark. Wilkes was imprisoned in the latter after winning the Middlesex election in 1768. His supporters demonstrated outside the prison, and on 10 May around 15,000 assembled crying 'Wilkes and Liberty!' They were shot at by fearful troops, killing seven demonstrators, in what became known as the 'Massacre of St George's Fields'.

Wilkes died in December 1797 in his Grosvenor Square house and was buried in a vault in the nearby Grosvenor Chapel, South Audley Street, Mayfair, W1.

There is a famous statue of Wilkes at the corner of New Fetter Lane and Fetter Lane, to the north of Fleet Street, EC4. Unveiled in October 1988, the statue displays his squint, thereby being claimed as the only cross-eyed statue in London.

Charles James Fox was born on 24 January 1749 in Conduit Street W1, where the family was temporarily in residence while their usual London home, Holland House (in what is now Holland Park) was being repaired. He had a remarkably varied political career, several times as a leading government minister from the 1770s up to his death in 1806. However, he is perhaps more famous as an opposition champion of parliamentary reform. Like Wilkes, he had a duel in Hyde Park, when he faced William Adam in November 1779.

His election campaigns famously dramatic, especially the 1784 campaign for the Westminster constituency. The portico of St Paul's Church, in Covent Garden, was frequently used for election hustings. The celebrated Georgiana, Duchess of Devonshire was an ardent Foxite, and was reputed to campaign for Fox by offering kisses to voters in the streets of Covent Garden.

Fox had many London addresses. He was based at 46 Clarges Street, Piccadilly, W1 in 1803-4 while campaigning against Addington's Tory Government, and the site (currently the 'Fox Club'), has a plaque. He also lived at 26 (now 9) South Street, Mayfair, W1 (later the site of Egyptian Embassy offices); in St James's Street, next to Brooks's Club, where he incurred huge gambling debts. At Almack's Club, 50 Pall Mall, SW1, he once played faro for eight hours, losing £11,000. When friends found him afterwards, quietly reading Herodotus in Greek, he explained, 'What else is there to do when a man has lost every-thing?'

Fox died in September 1806 in the Duke of Devonshire's villa, Chiswick House, Burlington Lane, W4, and was buried in the North Transept of Westminster Abbey, SW1 (where there is a memorial). There is a statue of Fox as a Roman senator holding the Magna Carta, in Bloomsbury Square, WC1, erected in 1816.

METROPOLITY

City Links A-Z

ALBERT HALL

The site at Kensington Gore, SW7 was once occupied by Gore House where William Wilberforce, the slavery abolitionist, lived in the early 19th century. Later, as the residence of Lady Blessington and Count d'Orsay, between 1836 and 1849, it became a major society centre. Wellington once visited and was delighted by a talking crow which said 'Up boys and at 'em'.

The Albert Hall was opened by Queen Victoria in March 1871 in the presence of Gladstone and Disraeli. It has been the venue of many political events, such as major speeches by the Tory leader, Arthur Balfour, during the second 1910 election, and two years later by his successor, Bonar Law, strongly attacking the Liberal Government. The 1929 Conservative Conference was also held there. In the early 20th century, political meetings were often interrupted by supporters of women's suffrage; one even hid in an organ pipe and sent strange wailing noises through a microphone.

BIRTHPLACES OF PARTIES

- Willis's Rooms (formerly Almack's Assembly Rooms, later Almack House) in King Street, St James's, SW1 was the scene of a famous meeting on 6 June 1859 of various non-Tory parliamentary factions, popularly deemed to be the birth of the Liberal Party.

- In Farringdon Street, EC4 is the site of the Congregational Memorial Hall where the Labour Representation Committee was formed on 27 February 1900 (marked by a GLC plaque), and where, at a conference following the general election in early 1906, the LRC became the Labour Party.

- David Owen's home at 78 Narrow Street, Limehouse, E14 was the location for the so-called 'Limehouse Declaration' by several leading dissident Labourites on 25 January 1981. This led on 26 March that year to the formation of the Social Democratic Party, which was formally launched at the Grand Hall of the Connaught Rooms, Great Queen Street, WC2.

BUCKINGHAM PALACE

The official London residence of the Sovereign since the mid-19th century. The Prime Minister has a weekly audience, and other government ministers can be seen entering and leaving the central gateway, especially when being appointed or removed from office.

Two interesting connections between the Sovereign and the government and Parliament concern the Vice-Chamberlain of the Household. This is a traditional Royal Household office held by one of the Government Whips. During the State Opening of Parliament the Vice-Chamberlain is 'held hostage' at Buckingham Palace, to ensure the Sovereign's safe return from Westminster. The Vice-Chamberlain writes a daily letter to the Sovereign, whenever Parliament is sitting, with all the relevant news of that day's parliamentary business.

CALL OF DUTY

In order that as many MPs and peers as possible can vote in parliamentary divisions, many sites near to the Palace of Westminster have a 'division bell' for the House of Commons and/or the House of Lords installed on their premises. To have such a facility is often regarded as quite a status symbol, and in order to be permitted to have one, an applicant must have the written support of six Members of Parliament.

Other than obvious locations such as government offices, party HQs, conference halls and private residences, many restaurants, pubs and hotels in the Westminster area have a division bell. These include the St Ermin's Hotel, Caxton Street; the St Stephen's Club, 34 Queen Anne's Gate; Shepherds Restaurant, Marsham Court; Albert Carvery Restaurant, 52 Victoria Street; Ritz Hotel, Piccadilly; Footstool Restaurant, St John's Smith Square, and the Royal Horseguards Hotel, Whitehall Place.

CITY SPEECHES

The heart of the City of London hosts annual speeches by senior government ministers:

- The Guildhall is the seat of the City of London's local government, the City Corporation, holding meetings of its Court of Common Council. The Great Hall is the scene of major gatherings, and boasts statues of Chatham, Pitt, Wellington and Churchill. It is also the venue for the annual Lord Mayor's Banquet each November, at which the Prime Minister traditionally makes a major speech.

- The Mansion House is the scene of the Chancellor of the Exchequer's speech at the Lord Mayor's annual dinner each June. One of the most famous was that of Lloyd George in 1911, which he used to warn Germany about its aggressive foreign policy, sparked by its sending of a gunboat to the Moroccan port of Agadir. The Foreign Secretary also makes a major speech at the Lord Mayor's Easter Banquet.

DUELS

In earlier times, political disputes would sometimes be settled by a duel. Some favoured sites were:

- Battersea Fields (now Battersea Park), SW11: The Duke of Wellington fought a duel with the Earl of Winchelsea over Catholic Emancipation on 21 March 1829. No-one was injured and honour was satisfied.

- Hyde Park: The Earl of Shelburne duelled with a Lt-Col Fullarton on 22 March 1780. He was wounded in the groin, but the affair made him very popular.

- Putney Heath, SW15: Pitt the Younger fought a duel on 27 March 1798 with a leading Whig, George Tierney, over a heated exchange in the Commons. Neither was harmed. The famous duel between two Cabinet ministers, George Canning and Viscount Castlereagh, also took place here, at 6am on 21 September 1809, over personal rivalry and jockeying for ministerial office. Canning was shot in the thigh.

- St James's Park: A favourite spot for duels in 18th century. William Pulteney and Lord Hervey duelled with swords on 25 January 1730, over the former's attacks on the latter's defence of Walpole

IRISH TROUBLES

London has suffered from many incidents connected with the history of Ireland. Bombs have caused many casualties and much damage, including recently Chelsea Barracks (October 1981), Hyde Park and Regent's Park (July 1982), Harrods (1983), Bishopsgate (April 1993) and Canary Wharf (February 1996).

36 Eaton Place, SW1 saw the murder of Sir Henry Wilson MP, former Chief of the Imperial Staff in 1920s by Irish terrorists on 22 June 1922. There was also an attempt on Edward Heath, when a two pound bomb was thrown from car outside his Wilton Street, Belgravia home, where he lived for a time after losing the premiership in 1974.

At Clerkenwell Prison, Clerkenwell Close, EC1, there was a failed attempt to free two Fenians in December 1867 by blowing up the prison wall. The explosion killed six locals. Michael Barrett was found guilty, and executed outside the walls of Newgate Prison (now Newgate Street, EC1), the last public execution in England.

LOCAL GOVERNMENT

As well as being a national capital, London is a city with a long history of municipal government. Outside the confines of the City itself (governed by the Corporation of London), there was a ramshackle system of local government for centuries as the metropolis grew. The London County Council was set up in the late 19th century (based at Spring Gardens, off Trafalgar Square, SW1), and in the 1960s was replaced by the Greater London Council and the 32 boroughs. From 1922 to 1986 the LCC and GLC were based at County Hall, SE1, a convenient location for the GLC's campaign against abolition in the mid-1980s, when the frontage was used for huge billboard messages to the parliamentarians at the Palace of Westminster just across the river.

Borough government in London has always been a lively affair. Poplar in East London became a byword for municipal socialism falling foul of the letter of the law in the 1920s, under the leadership of George Lansbury.

LONDON 'WHITE HOUSE'

Several US Presidents have connections in London other than in Grosvenor Square. John Quincy Adams, son of John Adams, was married at All Hallows by the Tower, St Dunstan's Hill, EC3. Martin van Buren lived at 7 Stratford Place, off Oxford Street, W1, in 1831-32. From 1902 to 1918 Herbert Hoover lived at 39 Hyde Park Gate, South Kensington, SW7.

Teddy Roosevelt married his second wife, Edith Kermit Carow, at St George's, Hanover Square W1 on 2 December 1886, describing himself as a 'ranchman'. They honeymooned in Brown's Hotel in Dover Street, W1, (as did his namesake, Franklin, in 1905).

John F. Kennedy lived at 14 Princes Gate, Knightsbridge SW7, when his father, Joseph, was the US ambassador. There is a memorial bust of JFK at the International Students Hostel, 1 Park Crescent, W1.

Other memorials to presidents include the George Washington statue in front of the National Gallery, Trafalgar Square, presented by the State of Virginia in 1921. There are statues of Abraham Lincoln in Parliament Square, presented by the American people in 1920, and at the Royal Exchange, City, EC3. FDR shares one of London's most amusing recent memorials, the sculpture ('The Allies') of Churchill and Roosevelt chatting on a bench in New Bond Street, W1.

MILITARY MANOEUVRES

One of the most famous political meetings in English constitutional history took place at St Mary's Church, Putney High Street, SW15, in October–November 1647. Cromwell's New

Model Army was based in Putney, and the Army Council used to discuss the future of the country around the communion table with their hats on.

POLITICAL DRINKING

Taverns and coffee houses (most long gone) were popular venues for meetings of political societies and clubs. The British Coffee House, 27 Cockspur Street, SW1 was the location for meetings of various political clubs, such as the Portland Club in 1791, and the Fox Club in January 1813. The Sutherland Arms tavern, May's Buildings, May's Court, WC2, was the meeting place of the Eccentrics Club, whose members included Sheridan, Fox and Melbourne. The Crown & Anchor pub in the Strand, WC2, saw the first London meeting of the famed Liberal reformer, John Bright, in 1842. The King's Head, Bowling Green Lane, Islington, EC1, was the venue for the first meeting of the London Patriotic Society in 1869. Meetings of the October Club, a Tory club, were held in the Bell Coffee House in King Street, Westminster, SW1.

At least two mock parliamentary clubs flourished in coffee houses. At the Crown Coffee House in Drury Lane, WC2, in the mid-18th century, were held meetings of the 'Flash Cove's Parliament' where each member took the title of a member of the Lords. The 'House of Lords Club', in the first half of the 19th century, started in the Fleece Tavern, Cornhill, EC3, then at the Three Tuns, Southwark and the Abercrombie Coffee House, Lombard Street, EC3. Its members were not peers, though they took pretend titles for themselves, and meetings were presided over by the 'Lord Chancellor' wearing legal wig and robes. There was a sliding scale of fees by title, e.g. 1/- for a baron, 5/- for a duke.

Queen's Hall, Langham Place

A major venue for political meetings of all kinds, including several party conferences, such as Labour in June 1923 and October 1924, and the Conservatives in 1912 (twice), 1922 and 1930.

It was here on 18 March 1931 that Stanley Baldwin, the Tory leader, attacked the Press lords over their campaigns against his policies, using a phrase suggested by his cousin, Rudyard Kipling. He described them as wanting "power without responsibility, the prerogative of the harlot throughout the ages".

Royal route

When the Sovereign goes to the Palace of Westminster for the State Opening of Parliament, the procession takes the following traditional route: Buckingham Palace – The Mall – Horse Guards Parade – Horse Guards Arch – Whitehall – Parliament Square – Palace of Westminster (Sovereign's Entrance). The State Opening usually takes place in November each year, although this may vary after a general election.

Somewhere private

Sometimes a private house is a convenient and sufficiently secret venue for especially sensitive meetings. For example, 96 Cheyne Walk, Chelsea, SW1 home of the then junior Northern Ireland minister, Paul Channon, was used for a meeting on 7 July 1972 between IRA and British Government representatives.

Tower of London

Various parts of the Tower have been used as a prison for 'enemies of the state'. After the 1660 Restoration, some of the accused regicides of Charles I were imprisoned here. Some died, while others were taken elsewhere and executed. Colonel Thomas Harrison, who had played a significant part in the trial and sentencing of the King, was executed at Charing Cross. Similar fates befell leading Jacobites including, in April 1747, Lord Lovat, the last person to be beheaded in England.

More recently Sir Roger Casement was held in St Thomas's Tower in 1916 before his treason trial, and Rudolf Hess was detained in the Governor's House for several days following his flight to Britain in 1941.

Two prime ministers had very different experiences of the Tower. In January 1712, Robert Walpole, accused of "high breach of trust and notorious corruption" when Secretary at War, was expelled from the Commons and imprisoned briefly in the Tower. While detained he still managed to receive many visitors. On the other hand, the Duke of Wellington was regarded as an active, successful Constable of the Tower (1824-52). He had the moat drained and the Wellington barracks built.

TRAFALGAR SQUARE

In the 19th century, this Square was the place for the airing of the grievances of parliamentary and social reformers. In the 20th century, the causes ranged from unemployment and women's suffrage to nuclear disarmament.

A demonstration by the unemployed on 8 February 1886 led to disturbances known as 'Black Monday'. On 13 November 1887 there was rioting following a protest by radical socialists and others, which became known as 'Bloody Sunday'. More recently, the Square saw some of its most intensive activity during the demonstrations against the introduction of poll tax in March 1990.

VARIOUS VENUES

• Caxton Hall, Caxton Street, SW1, was the site of many suffragette rallies, and of Liberal Party Assemblies in 1942 and 1950. At a Conservative Party meeting on 30 November 1930 to discuss policy on Empire Free Trade, the leader, Stanley Baldwin, said to the paparazzi as he went in: "photograph me now gentlemen; it may be the last time you will see me". In the register office, Anthony Eden was married to a niece of Winston Churchill in August 1952. Churchill himself is commemorated by a plaque for speaking at the Hall between 1937 to 1942.

• Clerkenwell Green, EC1, was a favourite place for large meetings and demonstrations. William Cobbett addressed an anti-Corn Law meeting there in February 1826 and Fergus

O'Connor spoke at a Chartist meeting in April 1848, a week before the famed Chartist march from Kennington Common.

- Conway Hall, Red Lion Square, WC1, is the home of the South Place Ethical Society and a popular venue for political events and meetings, often those not directly in the political mainstream.

- Kingsway Hall, 70 Great Queen Street, WC2, was the scene of a speech by the future Pakistan leader, Mohamed Jinnah, to the Muslim League in 1917, and a special Conservative Party Conference was held there in 1946.

- Speaker's Corner, Hyde Park, near Marble Arch, W1, is a traditional spot for anyone to speak on any subject. The right of assembly was established in 1872 as a result of public demonstrations mounted by the Reform League to campaign for a wider vote.

- St Ermin's Hotel, Caxton Street, SW1 has long been a popular meeting place for politicians because of its proximity to Westminster and Whitehall. The hotel has a division bell, and there is a passageway, now blocked up, that ran from under the main staircase to Parliament. It saw the launch of Conservative 'Yes' Campaign during the Common Market Referendum, and a two day meeting of Liberal MPs in June 1977to debate the continuation of their agreement with the then minority Labour Government, the 'Lib-Lab pact'.

- St James's Hall, Piccadilly, SW1, on the site of the later Piccadilly Hotel was the venue of the 1897 Conservative Party Conference.

WELLINGTON CORNER

There is so much information about the Duke of Wellington around Hyde Park Corner that it deserves to be renamed. The Wellington Arch dominates the roundabout, and his former home, Apsley House ('No. 1, London') is now the Wellington Museum. The pedestrian underpasses are lined with tiles telling his story, and the Achilles statue just inside Hyde Park commemorates his victories.

*Political Eating, Drinking and Shopping**

Westminster is somewhat of a culinary desert – at least that's its reputation. But there are a few oases in the desert, where one can sample anything from ordinary British pub food to the most exquisite five-star menu on offer in London.

RESTAURANTS & BARS

- The Atrium, 4 Millbank, London, SW1 (tel 020 7233 0032) is a top class restaurant located within the building that houses all the media organisations covering Parliament. As its name suggests it is situated in the central atrium of the whole building. Delightful airy surroundings together with the political buzz that makes Westminster such a lively place to work in. You're bound to spot a famous politician lunching with a political journalist, or a lobbyist schmoozing with a Minister. The food is excellent, if rather pricey (reckon to pay around £30-40 per person). But be prepared for some slow, but polite, service.

- Bar Excellence, 1 Abbey Orchard Street, SW1 (tel 020 7222 4707). Basement bar and restaurant just off Victoria Street by

* Compiled by John Simmons

the Department of Trade & Industry. Caters for a hip younger crowd and is decorated in very tasteful bright colours. Primarily a bar which serves excellent (and plentiful portions) of simple food, its restaurant is located on a mezzanine balcony above the bar. A superb atmosphere and great European food. Expect to pay about £20-£30 per head in the restaurant. Well worth a visit.

- Gran Paradiso, 52 Wilton Road, SW1 (tel 020 7828 5818) Popular with Conservative MPs despite the fact that it's quite a hike from the House of Commons – located near to Victoria Station. Wide ranging Italian menu and very reasonably priced.

- L'Amico, 44 Horseferry Road, SW1 (tel 020 7222 4680). Italian basement restaurant, a favourite with MPs and journalists. Walls are decorated with pictures of famous people (mainly politicians and foreign dignitaries) who have lunched there, including Mikhail Gorbachev!

- Shepherds Restaurant, Marsham Court, Marsham Street SW1 (tel 020 7834 9552). Probably the most exclusive and expensive restaurant in the Division Bell area surrounding Parliament. High class English fayre, so if you like your Roast Beef and Yorkshire Pudding followed by Spotted Dick, this is the place for you. Decor is classic English wood panelling with booths for privacy. Another good place to spot famous politicians.

- Olivo, 21 Eccleston Street, SW1 (tel 020 7730 2505). One of the best restaurants in London. Exquisite Italian and Mediterranean food. Quite small so advance booking is advisable. Service and presentation is excellent. Expect to pay £30-£40 per person.

- Kundan Indian Restaurant, 3 Horseferry Road, SW1 (tel 020 7834 3434). One of former Prime Minister John Major's favourite eateries. Basic Indian menu, this restaurant is particularly popular with backbenchers on a budget.

- Simply Nico, 48a Rochester Row, SW1 (020 7630 8061). One of London's finest restaurants with a superb (and expensive!) menu. If you want to impress someone (particularly with the size of your wallet) this is the place to take them.

- Politico's Coffee House, 8 Artillery Row, SW1 (tel 020 7828 0010). Small balcony coffee house located above Politico's Political Bookstore. Serves high class coffee and teas as well as sandwiches, quiches and delicious cakes. Ideal place for a snack break and to watch Parliament live on TV.

- Churchills, Whitehall, SW1. Cheap and cheerful sandwich bar located virtually opposite the entrance to Downing Street in Whitehall. Tony Blair sends out for his sandwiches here!

- Red Lion Pub, 48 Parliament Street, SW1. Rough and ready pub which is popular among political journalists and civil servants. Located opposite the entrance to Downing Street.

- The Speaker Pub, Great Peter Street, SW1. Newly refurbished pub, decorated with pictures of various Speakers of the House of Commons.

- Marquis of Granby Public House 41 Romney Street, SW1. Used to be a haven of left wing intrigue, located as it was next to Transport House, the former home of the Labour Party and TGWU. They have both since moved but it still has that conspiratorial feel to it. Nowadays frequented by staff from nearby Conservative Central Office.

- Westminster Arms, Storey's Gate, SW1. Located to the side of the hideous Queen Elizabeth II Conference Centre, this pub is popular with tourists and politicos alike.

SHOPS

- Politico's Bookstore & Coffee House, 8 Artillery Row, SW1 (020 7828 0010). Located just off Victoria Street by the Army & Navy Department Store, this is Britain's only specialist political bookstore. Politico's stocks a huge range of political books, magazines, think tank reports as well as political gift items, memorabilia, cartoon, videos and tapes. There is also a mezzanine coffee house where you can sip fine coffees and watch Parliament live on TV.

- Parliamentary Bookshop, 12 Bridge Street, SW1 (020 7219 3890). Located on the corner of Parliament Square and Whitehall, the Parliamentary Bookshop specialises in Government publications and books on Parliament.

- Church House Bookshop, 31 Great Smith Street, SW1 (020 7898 1301). Specialist religious bookshop. Well worth a visit.

POLITICAL
LONDON
QUIZ

Questions

Q1. Which famous twentieth century nationalist leader worked
(a) as a dishwasher and apprentice pastry-cook in a Haymarket hotel?
(b) as Post Office savings bank clerk?

Q2. Which small central London street was described by Dickens in his novel *Nicholas Nickleby* as 'a street of gloomy lodging houses ... a sanctuary of smaller Members of Parliament ... There are legislators in the parlours, in the first floor, in the second, in the third, in the garrets; the small apartments reek with the breath of deputations and delegates'?

Q3. Where in central London was said to get its name from a king walking his dogs and was the site of a fatal accident when a prime minister fell off his horse?

Q4. (a) Which famous politician was Guilford Street, WC1 named after?
(b) Which central London street was, at one point, proposed to be named after the Duke of Wellington?
(c) Which hotel boasts the Chartwell Suite and Library and Clementine's Restaurant?

Q5. Which future Prime Minister attended the appropriately named Mr Gladstone's Day School near Sloane Square, SW1?

Q6. Which famous twentieth century political cartoonists lived at the following addresses, both marked by an English Heritage plaque:
(a) 33 Melbury Court, Kensington High Street, W8?
(b) Welbeck Mansions, New Cavendish St, W1?

Q7. What do the following London suburbs have in common: Orpington, Leyton, Bermondsey and Mitcham & Morden?

Q8. In what Belgravia square lived politicos as diverse as Metternich, Tory premiers Baldwin, Chamberlain, Heath and Thatcher, and Liberal PMs Russell and Campbell Bannerman, and was for a time the temporary home of the Speaker following the destruction by fire of the old Palace of Westminster in 1834?

Q9. Who or what was 'Selsdon Man'?

Q10. Where can you see large concentrations of politicians in one place:
(a) in oils?
(b) in wax?
(c) in stone?
(d) on mugs, badges, cards etc.?

Answers

Q1. (a) Ho Chi Minh, the future Vietnamese revolutionary leader, worked in the Carlton Hotel, Haymarket, SW1 (later New Zealand House) in 1913, in the kitchen of the celebrated French chef, Escoffier. A plaque erected by the British Vietnam Association marks this surprisingly domestic piece of history.
(b) Michael Collins, the Irish nationalist, was a clerk for the West Kensington PO Savings Bank while living at 5 Netherwood Road, south of Shepherd's Bush, W14 in the early years of last century, where there is a commemorative plaque by Kensington & Chelsea Council.

Q2. Canon Row, Westminster, SW1. It runs north from Bridge Street, opposite the Palace of Westminster, and is now no longer a public thoroughfare, being flanked by parliamentary offices, including the new Portcullis House. It used to be called Cannon Row, but in recent years reverted to its original spelling.

Q3. Constitution Hill, SW1. The name probably comes from Charles II's constitutional walks with his spaniels. Sir Robert Peel was thrown from his horse here in 1850 and later died from his injuries.

Q4. (a) Lord North, the Conservative PM of the late 18th century, who became the 2nd Earl of Guilford in 1790.
(b) Regent's Park. There were suggestions in the press that it be named after Wellington, and a villa was designed and exhibited at the Royal Academy the following year where he might live in the Park.

(c) The Churchill Inter-Continental Hotel, 30 Portman Square, W1. It also has a Churchill Bar and Divan.

Q5. Harold Macmillan, from 1900-1903. He was born, and lived as a child, at nearby 52 Cadogan Place.

Q6. (a) David Low
(b) Victor Weisz, better known as 'Vicky'.

Q7. They were all the sites of significant by-elections in the second half of the last century. In Orpington in March 1962, the Liberal Eric Lubbock captured what was a Conservative stronghold with a huge swing. It was the most sensational by-election result for 30 years, and marked the start of a Liberal revival. Patrick Gordon Walker, who had been made Foreign Secretary in the new Labour Government in October 1964 despite losing his Smethwick seat in the general election, surprisingly failed to secure his return to Parliament in a by-election in Leyton the following January in what was supposed to be a safe Labour seat. He was forced to resign his Cabinet seat, which cut Labour's already slender Commons majority even further. The Mitcham & Morden by-election in June 1982 was the only one to result directly from the creation of the Social Democratic Party. The former Labour MP, Bruce Douglas-Mann, chose to seek re-election following his defection to the SDP, but lost the by-election to the Conservatives, who were enjoying their post-Falklands War revival. The disastrous Labour showing in the June 1983 general election was presaged by its humiliation in the Bermondsey by-election the previous February, where a supposedly solid Labour docklands constituency fell to the Liberal Simon Hughes following a bitter and divisive campaign.

Q8. Eaton Square, SW1

Q9. In January 1970 leading Conservatives met at the Selsdon Park Hotel, Croydon Road, Croydon for a pre-election policy session, producing a programme which was seen by some as a break from the so-called post-war consensus. It led to Prime Minister Harold Wilson's famous reference to 'Selsdon Man' in a speech at a London Labour Party rally at Camden Town Hall, Euston Road, WC1 a few weeks later, an attempt to portray the Conservatives as uncaring right-wing extremists.

Q10. (a) The National Portrait Gallery, St Martin's Place, off Trafalgar Square, WC2 has an excellent collection of paintings (and busts) of politicians past and present
(b) Madame Tussaud's, Marylebone, NW1 exhibits life-sized wax statues of many famous political figures
(c) The Parliament Square area, including the Palace of Westminster and Westminster Abbey
(d) Politico's Bookstore, Artillery Row, SW1 (of course!)

INDEX OF
NAMES & PLACES